The
Purejoojoo
Guide to the
Understanding

The Understanding of Everything
Your Mind Can Do For You Too

ISABEL MAR

The Purejoojoo Guide to the Understanding
Isabel Mar

ISBN: 978-0-9863462-3-1 (hardcover)
ISBN: 978-0-9863462-4-8 (trade paperback)
ISBN: 978-0-9863462-5-5 (ebook)

Cover art: Gonzalo Martín Rodríguez
Pre-press: Lighthouse24

Learn more at www.purejoojoo.com

This book is dedicated to You.

Who you are.

Not who you think you should be.

Contents

1. The Where

The reason why you feel stuck right now is because you are.
You are stuck in a thought.
You.
Who you are.
And you are not a thought.

It is the Thought that makes you think Life is doing anything
to you.
Yet Life just is.

It is the Thought that makes you think you never have
enough Time.
Yet Time passes at the same time for all of us.

And it is the Thought that makes you think you need to be
more than who you already are.
Yet you are not a thought.

You simply are.

And you are enough.
Just the way you are.

You have always been enough.
As you are.

Which is why there is only one you.
Because only you can do what only you can do.

Be you.

Which is why no one else can be who you are.
Because you are enough.

You have always been enough.
Because there is such thing as Enough.

Because you are enough.
Just the way you already are too.

The reason why you keep struggling is because you keep struggling against you.

And you are not a thought.

You simply learned to think about you.
Because we all do.

Because our minds think.
Your mind thinks too.

Which is how you learned to think about you as a self.
Your self.

Rather than as you.
Who you are.

Your self is a thought.
An image you created of you.

Of who you think you should be.
Of what you think you should be too.

In order to be accepted.
In order to be approved.

In order to be seen.
In order to be heard.

In order to be liked.
In order to be loved.

Even by you.

Because your self is a thought.
An image.

An image that constantly needs to be maintained.
An image that constantly needs to be improved.

Which is why you feel tired right now.
Because it is tiring to maintain this image.

Why you feel exhausted right now too.
Because it is exhausting to keep thinking you need to be
something other than you.

Which is why you no longer see what you are doing.
You no longer see what your own thoughts are doing to you.

Your thoughts create a reality.
Your own reality about you.

Which you then project onto others.
And project onto Life too.

So you no longer see it as it is.
You no longer see you as you are too.

You see it as a thought.
Your own thought about you.

Which is how you learned to think Life is doing something to you.
How you learned to think someone is doing something to you too.

Because this is what your own thoughts are doing.
This is what your own thoughts are doing to you.

Which is how you learned to think people are judging you.
Because this is what your own thoughts are doing too.

Judging you.
Against who you think you should be.

Which is how you learned to think you need to keep comparing.
Because this is what your own thoughts are doing too.

Comparing you to an ideal, a standard, an expectation.
An expectation you created of you.

Which makes you think this is what people are doing to you too.

So when you look in the mirror, you no longer see who you are.
You are seeing the thought.
Your own thought being reflected back to you.

The thought you learned that makes you see everything wrong.

Which is why you see every imperfection.
Every flaw.
Everything wrong about you.

Which is how you learned to think it is never enough.
Because your own thoughts make you think this way too.

Which is why nothing is ever enough.
Why you no longer think you are enough.
Why you no longer think Enough is enough.

Which is how you learned to think there is such thing as a
better you.
Because you think you need to be better too.

Better than everyone else.
Better than who you already are too.

Which is why you keep struggling.
Because you keep struggling against you.

And you are enough.
Simply being who you are.
Simply being you.

Your mind simply got conditioned to think.
Think these patterns of thoughts that keep you thinking the
way you do.
Think these patterns of thoughts that keep you thinking
about you.

Rather than being who you are too.

Which is how you learned to forget.
Forget about you.
Who you already are too.

Because you are always in a thought.

Thinking of who you think you should be.
Thinking of where you think you need to be.
Thinking of how you think you want it to be too.

And when you are in a thought, you are no longer here.
Because *you* are in a thought.

In a thought that keeps you back there.
Tied to an experience that has already passed.

Or over there.
Tied to an experience that may never happen.

Either way, you are no longer here.

Which is why you feel lost.
Because you are.
You are lost in your thoughts.

Why you feel split.
Divided.
Disconnected.

Because you are disconnected from you.
Who you are.
Because you are not a thought.

So you no longer hear you.
Because all you hear right now is what your thoughts are
saying to you.

Thoughts that make you think you need to be more.
Do more.
Have more.

Thoughts that make you think you are always at fault.
Thoughts that make you think you are never to blame.
Thoughts that make you think you are always right.
Thoughts that make you think you are never wrong.

So you no longer hear what is being said.
Because you hear it through your own thought.

Thoughts that criticize.
Thoughts that blame.
Thoughts that punish.
Thoughts that shame.

Which is why you hear everything now as a criticism, an attack, a disappointment, something you lack.

Which is why two people can say the exact same words.
Yet you hear it in a completely different way.

When a friend or a child says it, you hear it as it is.
A question.
A comment.
An observation.

When a parent or a spouse says it, you hear it as a thought.

So it is no longer just a question.
You hear it as someone telling you what to do.
Because this is what your own thoughts are doing too.

It is no longer just a comment.
You hear it as a disapproval.
Because this is what your own thoughts are doing to you.

It is no longer an observation.
You hear it as yet another way you have fallen short.
Because this is what your own thoughts keep saying to you too.

So you forget how to listen.
How to listen to what you have to say too.

Because all you hear right now are your thoughts.

Rather than the voice inside of you.
Your voice.
Your own voice for you.

That simply knows who you are.
That simply knows what you want to do.
And what you need too.

So you no longer feel how you do.
Because all you feel right now is your thoughts.
How your thoughts make you feel about you.

Your feelings are natural.
Your feelings are true.

Because your feelings are a direct reflection of you.

Which is why you don't think to cry.
You just do.

Why you don't think to laugh.
You just do.

And right now, you no longer allow you to feel how you do.

Which is why you no longer allow you to rest.
Even when you feel tired.

You no longer allow you to sit.
Even when you feel exhausted.

You no longer allow you to simply be.

Simply be here.
With you.
Who you are.
Who you have always been too.

Because you think it will hurt too much.

Because right now, all you know about you is your thoughts.

Thoughts you learned to think about you.
Thoughts that make you think it was because of you too.

Something you did.
Something you said.
Something you are.

Thoughts that make you think you are a sinner.
Thoughts that make you think you are broken.
Thoughts that make you think you are no longer worthy and
deserving as you are too.

So your mind keeps thinking this way about you.

Which makes you see things the way you do.
Which makes you hear things and feel things the way you do
too.

Which is why you feel heavy right now.

Because the Heaviness is the weight of your thoughts.

All the thoughts you carry around with you.
Thoughts you learned to think about you.
Thoughts someone else made you learn to think about you
too.

Yet you are not a thought.

You simply are.
And you are here.
You have always been here.

Right here.

Exactly where you need to be.
Exactly where you want to be too.

2. The What

The reason why you are exactly where you need to be is because it is the only way you could have arrived here.

The reason why you are exactly where you want to be is because it is the only way you would have arrived here.

And where you are is at the Understanding.
Because it always begins from the Understanding.

Because one Moment of Understanding can change your entire life.

From what you thought it was.
To what it is too.

From who you thought you were.
To who you simply are too.

You simply couldn't see what you were doing.
So you couldn't see what you were doing to you.

Because you weren't supposed to yet.

Because it is the only way you could have arrived.
It is the only way you would have arrived here too.

Because you needed to be ready.

Ready to be responsible.
Responsible for you.

Responsible for your own thoughts.
Responsible for your own mind too.

Because you are the master of your own mind.
Your thoughts don't master you.

Your mind simply got conditioned to think in certain ways.

Before you could understand.
Before you could understand who you are.
Before you could understand what you are doing too.

Because this is how it is for all of us.
This is how it is for you too.

Which is why it is called the Human Condition.

Because all of our minds get conditioned to think about who
we are.
Your mind got conditioned to think about who you are too.

Which is why we all get stuck in our thoughts.
Why you got stuck in your own thoughts too.

Because we are all doing the same thing.
You are doing the same thing too.

And what we are all doing is experiencing who we are for the
first time.
You are experiencing who you are for the first time too.

The Experience of Who We Are.
The Experience of Who You Are too.

The Experience of You.

Which is how we can all relate.
How you can relate too.

Relate to the Pain of thinking you are no longer enough as you are.
Relate to the Shame of thinking you no longer feel you are enough too.

Relate to the Blame of thinking someone did you wrong.
Relate to the Guilt of thinking you did something wrong too.

Relate to the Loneliness of thinking no one understands.
Relate to the Suffering of thinking you don't understand too.

Because we are all experiencing who we are for the first time.
And so are you.

Which is why you are never alone.
Because you are experiencing it too.

Because you are never alone in the thoughts you think about you.
Because we have all thought the same thoughts about who we are too.

Which is why we all struggle.
Why you are struggling right now too.

Because right now, the Experience of You has simply been limited to your thoughts.
Your own thoughts about you.

So you no longer know who you are.
You no longer know *you*.

So the Balance is lost.

Thoughts limit.
Limit what it is to a Thought.
Rather than everything it is too.

Your own thoughts limit you.
To your own thoughts about you.

So you no longer see everything you are.
You no longer see the Wholeness of You.

Which is why you feel unbalanced.
Unsteady.
Unrooted.

Because your entire experience got rooted in a Thought.
A thought about you.

Before you could understand.
Before you could understand for you too.

Which is how you learned to think that one experience
defines who you are.
Which is why you have this limited view of you.

So every experience gets blocked by this Thought.
Every experience in the Experience of You.

So the Balance is lost.

The Balance is not the opposite.
The Balance is in the Wholeness.

Because the Wholeness includes you.
Because you are included too.

Everything in Life has a Balance.
To make it whole.

A Day is completed from the day.
And the night too.

This is the Balance.
This is the Wholeness.
The Wholeness of a Day.

Simply how a Day is.
Simply how your day is too.

Life is completed from the living.
And the dying too.

This is the Balance.
This is the Wholeness.
The Wholeness of Life.

Simply how Life is.
Simply how your life is too.

You are completed from your understanding.
The Understanding of Who You Are.
The Understanding of You.

This is the Balance.
This is the Wholeness.
The Wholeness of You.

Because you are already complete.
As you.

Simply how it is.
Simply how you are too.

You simply learned to think you are no longer complete.
As you are too.

Because this is simply how the Experience is for all of us.
This is how the Experience of You is too.

Because our minds got conditioned to think.

Think we need to be something other than who we are.
Your mind got conditioned to think you need to be something
other than who you are too.

Which is why you think there is something missing.

Because there is.

You are missing you.

All you need to complete is you.

The Understanding of Who You Are.
The Understanding of You.

When you learn to forget about you, your mind gets
conditioned to think it is selfish when you do it for you too.

Because you no longer see you.
How you are someone too.

It is only selfish when you only do it for you.
Because the Balance is lost.

When you do it for you too, you return to the Balance.
Because you see the Wholeness.

Because you see it too.

How you matter.
How you are included.
How the Wholeness includes you too.

So you feel balanced.
You feel whole.
Because you are doing it for you too.

Which is why you start to feel resentful, unappreciated,
overlooked when you only do it for others.
Because the Balance is lost.

Why you start to feel uninspired, disengaged, isolated when
you only do it for you.
Because the Balance is lost too.

The Balance is not the opposite.
The Balance is in the Wholeness.

And the Wholeness includes you.
Because you are included too.

And right now, the Balance is lost.

Which is how you got stuck.

Your mind simply learned to think in terms of opposites.
Which keeps you stuck in another thought.

This or that.
Yes or no.
Should I or shouldn't I.

The constant back and forth.
From one thought to another.

So your mind simply didn't know what else to do.
Your mind simply didn't know what else you wanted it to do
for you too.

Because you weren't supposed to yet.

Because you always get to choose.
You always get to choose how you want to experience you.

As a thought that continues to blame, pity and victimize you.
Or as you.

Responsible for who you are.
Responsible for what your own thoughts are doing too.

Because your mind can also do this.
Your mind can do this for you too.

To understand what you are doing.
To understand what you can do for you too.

Which is why it always begins from the Understanding.

Because one Moment of Understanding can change the entire
Experience.

One moment of your own understanding can change the
entire Experience of You.

From what you thought it was.
To everything it has always been for you too.

3. The Why

The reason why you didn't know what else your mind could
do is because you weren't supposed to yet.

Because We Are All Still Learning.
You are still learning too.

Learning everything your mind can also do.
Learning everything your own mind can do for you too.

The Mind thinks.
Your mind thinks too.

Simply how the Mind is.
Simply how your mind is too.

What you haven't learned yet is how the Mind can also
receive.
How your mind can receive too.

Receive the Understanding.

To heal the thoughts you learned to think about you.
To release the thoughts someone else made you learn to think
about you too.

So your mind can simply be.

Be at peace.
So you can be at peace too.

And the only way for the Mind to receive is when it is empty.
The only way for your mind to receive is when it is empty too.

Empty of all thought.
Empty to receive.

Because when the Mind is receiving, it is no longer thinking.
When your mind is receiving, it is no longer thinking about
you.

Because when your mind is receiving the Understanding, it is
no longer about you.
It is for you too.

For you to understand the Why.
For you to understand the reason why you are worthy and
deserving to receive too.

Worthy and deserving to receive the Understanding.
To understand why it happened.
To understand why it happened for you too.

To settle your mind.
To make peace with your own mind too.

Because when you understand, your mind is settled.
Because you understand.

So you no longer need to think about it.
You no longer need to think about you.

Because it makes sense.
It makes sense for you too.

So you can be released.
So you can break through too.

Break the cycle of thoughts.
Break the endless loop too.

Because the Struggle *is* the Thought.
The Understanding is the Release.

Which is why your mind kept racing.
Why your mind kept spinning.
Why your mind kept going.

Because your mind simply didn't know what else you wanted it to do.
Other than think.

Because you are still learning.
We Are All Still Learning too.

Learning everything the Mind is.
Everything your own mind is too.

Because you are the master of your own mind.
Your thoughts don't master you.

You simply learned to see your mind as a thought.

Which is how you learned to think of your mind as your own worst enemy.
Rather than as your best friend too.

Because you simply didn't know your mind could also receive.
Receive the Understanding for you too.

This is the Balance.
This is the Wholeness.
This is the Wholeness of everything your mind can do too.

So you can see the Wholeness.
The Wholeness of every experience in the Experience of You.

To see how every experience didn't just happen to you.
Every experience happened for you too.

To arrive at the Understanding of what else your mind can also do.
To return to the Understanding of how your mind has always been here for you too.

To complete the Understanding of why it happened.
To complete the Understanding of who you are too.

To return you to who you are.
To return you to the Understanding of You.

Everything in Life is a natural cycle of Arriving and Returning.

The day arrives and returns.
The seasons arrive and return.

You have already arrived.
And it is your choice to choose to return.

To keep returning to the Understanding.
To return you here.

Right here.

Exactly where you are.
Exactly where you need to be too.

So your mind can return to its natural state of being.

Being still.
Being silent.
Being empty to receive.

So you can return to your natural state of being too.

Being still.
Being silent.
Being empty to receive.

Receive everything Life has to offer.
Receive everything your life has to offer you too.

Because when your mind is empty, you are open.
Open to all the possibilities.

Because when your mind is empty, you are open to receive.

The difference between when the Mind is thinking and when it is receiving is how it makes you feel.

The difference between when your mind is thinking and when it is receiving is how it makes you feel about you.

Which is why you feel tense right now.
Uneasy.
Insecure.

Because your mind got filled.
Filled with thoughts.

Thoughts that fill you with fear and dread.
Thoughts that keep you stuck in your head.

Which is why you feel tired and exhausted.

Because it is tiring to carry this weight around with you.
It is exhausting to place so much weight on what other people think too.

Which is why you can't relax.

Because it is unnatural.
It is unnatural for your mind to always be thinking.
It is unnatural for your mind to always be on.

So the Balance is lost.

And when the Balance is lost, it means there is Force.
Because you are forcing it to be something other than how it simply is.
You are forcing you to be someone other than who you simply are.

And you already are.
You already are who you are.

Because you already are you.

And you already are enough.
Just the way you already are too.

Because it is only natural to be you.

Which is why no one else can be who you are.
No one else can be you.

Which is why you still don't understand why you can't just be who you are too.

So your mind keeps thinking.
Thinking about why you can't just be you.

Which is why you can't stop your mind from thinking.
Because you simply haven't learned yet how your mind can receive the Understanding too.

The Understanding of Who You Are.
The Understanding of You.

When your mind is receiving, you feel calm and at ease.
Because you are relaxed.
Relaxed in your own being.

Because your mind is empty.
So you can simply listen.
Simply listen and receive.

Receive the Understanding.

To understand how to stop the constant chatter.
To understand how you have always mattered.

Until the Mind learns how to receive, you will be stuck in another thought.

Until your mind learns how to receive, you will be stuck in another thought about you.

Which is why someone can tell you over and over again how much they love you.

But until your mind learns how to receive it, you will keep blocking it with a thought.

A thought that makes you think you are no longer deserving to be loved as you.
A thought that makes you think there are conditions before you can be loved by you too.

Which is why you push away the ones you love.
Why you push away your own love too.

Which is why repeating the same thought over and over again never breaks the cycle.
Because you are still in a thought.

A thought that makes you think about you.
Because you are convincing you.
Rather than understanding why you are too.

Until your mind receives the Understanding, you still need to think about it.
Because you still don't have the Understanding.
The reason why.

Which is why you can lose the physical weight.
And still carry the weight of all your thoughts.

Why you can attain everything you thought would make you happy.
And still be miserable.

Because you still don't understand why you are worthy and deserving too.

Worthy and deserving to receive the Peace, the Calm, the Comfort in your life.

Worthy and deserving to receive the Lightness and Joy in your life too.

Until you receive the Understanding of why you are already worthy and deserving too, you will keep fighting it with a thought.

Until you receive the Understanding of how you are already worthy and deserving too, you will keep fighting it with your own thought about you.

Which is why every thought is learned.
Every single one.

Because anything learned can be unlearned and relearned.

Anything.

Because you always get to choose.

You always get to choose what you want to do with your own mind.
Because your mind can learn how to do what you want it to do for you too.

Because your mind can learn a new daily practice.
So you can experience what it means for you too.

The Meaning of You.

Why you are worthy.
Why you are deserving.
Why you matter.
Why you are here too.

To focus the Mind on the Understanding.
To focus your mind on your own understanding too.

To shift from the Thinking to the Understanding.
To understand why you are too.

To break the habit your mind learned how to do.
To break the daily habit your mind learned how to do to you.

The daily habit of thinking about you.
The daily habit of overanalyzing and overreacting too.

To break the old patterns of thought that limit you from
seeing everything it is.

To break you out of the old patterns of conditioning that limit
you from seeing everything you are too.

To allow the Mind to empty.
To allow the Mind to settle too.

So your mind can settle.
So you can be settled too.

To return you to the Peace.
The Peace of the Mind.
The peace of your own mind too.

To return you to the Calm.
The Calm of the Body.
The calm of your own body too.

To return you to the Comfort.
The Comfort of the Being.
The comfort of your own being too.

Simply being.
Being here.
In the comfort of who you are too.

So you can simply be.

Your natural state of being.
Being relaxed in who you are.
Being at ease as you are too.

Being relaxed with how it is.
Being at ease with how it simply is.
And how you are right now too.

Which is why you still have Moments of Lightness and Joy.
Because you are always here.
Waiting patiently for you to return here too.

To learn how to receive the Understanding.
Because the Understanding is always here too.

For your mind to learn how to receive.
So you can learn how to receive too.

Receive everything that has always been here.
Waiting patiently for you to receive this Understanding for
you too.

Which is why it always begins from the Understanding.

Because one Moment of Understanding can change how you
see the Mind.

One moment of your own understanding can change how you
see your own mind too.

To see how you are the master of your own mind.
Your thoughts don't master you.

4. The How

And this is How.
How you do it for you too.

How to master your own mind.
Rather than allow your thoughts to master you.

The How is your Daily Purejoojoo Practice.

A daily practice to shift from the Thinking to the
Understanding.
For your mind to learn how to receive the Understanding too.

So you can receive everything that has always been here.
To see how you have always been worthy and deserving to
receive it for you too.

Your Daily Purejoojoo Practice has three parts:
1. A morning practice.
2. An afternoon practice.
3. An evening practice.

1. Every morning, this is what you will do:

Read the Understanding in your mind.

At the end of the guide are journal pages.
Each page has an Understanding for you too.
So your mind learns how to receive.
Receive the Understanding of Who You Are.
Receive the Understanding of How It Simply Is Too.
So you understand everything your mind can do.
Everything your own mind can do for you too.

Then receive Three Full Cycles of Breath.

So you can feel it.
How it feels to be complete.
Completed by you.
Being completely here.
Being completely present.
In the Presence of Who You Are.
Who you already are too.

2. Every afternoon, this is what you will do:

At 3:00 p.m., you will simply listen and receive.

Listen to the Three Minute Purejoojoo Guided Breathing
Experience.
To experience what it means to empty your mind.
To experience how your mind can simply be empty too.
To relax into your being.
Being here.
Being you.

3. Every evening, this is what you will do:

Write out the Understanding.

So you can see it.
So your mind can see it too.
See how the Understanding makes sense.
How it makes sense for you too.

Then read the Understanding out loud.

With your own voice.
So your mind can hear it.
So you can hear it too.

Then receive Three Full Cycles of Breath.

So you can feel it.
Your breath.
Your presence.
So you can feel you.

Before you begin, let's take a moment to understand how to receive your own breath.
So your mind understands too.

The Breath comes from the Belly.
Because you came from the belly too.

Because when you breathe from your belly, it passes through your heart.
So you can feel it too.

Because you are feeling you.

How you arrived.
How you can always return too.

To see how you are always supported.
How your breath is always supporting you.

To clear your mind of all thought.
To empty your mind of all thoughts too.

Because your mind is no longer thinking.
It is no longer thinking about you.

It is receiving the Understanding.
The Understanding of how to breathe for you too.

To breathe you back to Life.
From all the thoughts that made you feel numb inside of you.

So let's begin.

Find a quiet place and lay down on your back.
Arms by your side.
Palms facing up.

With your eyes closed, start to relax.
Relax your feet.
Relax your toes.
Relax your legs.
Relax your arms.
Relax your hands.
Relax your fingers.
Relax your face.
Relax your breath.

And simply listen and receive.

Inhale through the nose – filling the belly up – for 4 – 5 and 6.
Exhale through the nose – letting it all go – for 4 – 5 and 6.

Inhale – 2 – 3 – 4 – 5 and 6.
Exhale – 2 – 3 – 4 – 5 and 6.

Inhale – big belly – big balloon – for 4 – 5 and 6.
Exhale – nice and easy – nice and slow – for 4 – 5 and 6.

The Breath comes from the belly.
Not the chest.

The Breath comes in through the nose and out through the nose.
To complete one full cycle.
To complete the natural cycle of you.

Because you are already complete.
And when you are here, you see it.
You hear it.
You feel it too.

Breathe in – 2 – 3 – 4 – 5 and 6.
Breathe out – 2 – 3 – 4 – 5 and 6.

Breathe in – filling the belly up – for 4 – 5 and 6.
Breathe out – release – relax – for 4 – 5 and 6.

Breathe in – 2 – 3 – 4 – 5 and 6.
Breathe out – 2 – 3 – 4 – 5 and 6.

Once you have completed all the journal pages, you will have completed one full cycle of learning.

So your mind understands what else it can do when the thought arrives.
Because your mind understands how the Understanding will arrive too.

To return to the Peace, the Calm, the Comfort of the Understanding.
The Lightness and the Joy as you continue to receive your own understanding too.

Because every day you do your Daily Purejoojoo Practice, you are expanding the Mind.
Every day you do your Daily Purejoojoo Practice for you too, you are expanding your own mind too.

To include the Understanding.

The Understanding of how you are worthy and deserving to receive the Understanding too.

The Understanding of Who You Are.
Not who you think you are.
Not who someone else made you think you are too.

Because we all deserve to understand.
We all deserve to be understood too.

Which is why your Daily Purejoojoo Practice is based in Three Understandings.

To understand how it simply is.
To understand how it simply is for you too.

The Three Understandings are:
1. Simply Allow It To Arrive.
2. Simply Listen and Receive.
3. Simply Be.

And the only way to understand how to Simply Allow It To Arrive is to simply allow it to arrive.
The only way to understand how to Simply Listen and Receive is to simply listen and receive.
And the only way to understand how to Simply Be is to simply be.

Because the Mind will always have thoughts.
Your mind will always have thoughts too.

Because everything in Life is a natural cycle.
A natural cycle of Arriving and Returning.

Because the thoughts will arrive.
The thoughts will return.

Simply how the Mind is.
Simply how your mind is too.

But now the Understanding will also arrive.

To break the endless cycle.
To stop the broken record.
To avoid the downward spiral.

To keep returning to the Understanding too.

The Understanding of everything the Mind can do.
The Understanding of everything your own mind can do too.

So rather than fight against how the Mind simply is, simply allow the thoughts to arrive.
Rather than fight against how your mind simply is, simply allow your own thoughts to arrive too.

So you can stop fighting against how it simply is.
You can stop fighting how you simply are too.

So simply allow.

Simply allow the thought to arrive.
And it will.

Then simply listen and receive.
Receive the Understanding you have been practicing for you too.

When you do your Daily Purejoojoo Practice.
When you do it for you too.

So your mind can settle.
And be empty too.

So your mind can simply be.
So you can simply be here too.

Released from the Thought.
Released from your own thought too.

To return to this Moment.
To be in this moment with you.

To learn how to receive.
Receive the gift you have been given too.

The Gift of the Understanding.
The gift of your own understanding too.

So you can see.
See it for you too.

See how no one is doing anything to you.

It is your own thought that is making you think the way you do.
It is your own thought that is making you do what you do.

And it is your own thought that can return you to the Understanding too.

Because the only time your mind gets to practice is when a thought arrives.
The only time your mind gets to practice is when your own thought arrives about you.

When you think someone is doing something to you.
When you think Life is doing something to you too.

Because the only time you need to receive the Understanding
is when you get stuck in a thought.
The only time you need to receive your own understanding is
when you get stuck in your own thought about you.

So rather than be afraid to be alone with your thoughts, you
see the gift your own thoughts are giving you too.

The gift to receive the Understanding of everything your mind
can also do.
The gift to receive your own understanding of how to master
your own mind too.

So you no longer allow one thought to ruin your entire day.
You no longer allow one experience to define the entire
Experience of You.

Because you understand.

You understand how to do it.
You understand how to do it for you too.

So every day, this is what you can choose to do.
Every day, this is what you can choose to do with your own
mind too.

Receive the Gift of the Understanding.
To learn how to receive your own understanding too.

To be at peace.

At peace with your own mind.
At peace with who you are.
At peace with how it is too.

So you can hear.
Hear it for you too.

Your own voice.
The voice inside of you.

That simply knows who you are.
And what you know you want to do for you too.

Guiding you back to who you are.
And everything you know you were meant to do too.

Because every time you release the thought, you are standing up for you.
Every time you release your own thought, you are speaking up for you too.

You are standing up to your own thoughts.
The thoughts that don't even make sense to you.

You are speaking up for you.
From your own understanding too.

So you can simply listen and receive.
Listen to what you have to say too.

Because you are no longer listening to the voices inside your head.
You are listening to you.

And receiving the Understanding for you too.

So you can trust again.
You can trust you.

And how you feel.
How your feelings are guiding you.

Because you feel it.
You feel you.

The Peace.
The Calm.
The Comfort.
The Lightness and the Joy too.

So you can decide.
You can decide what you want to do too.

How you want to experience your own life.
How you want to experience your own mind too.

And it takes Time.
It takes your own time too.

Which is why your Daily Purejoojoo Practice is a daily
practice.
To understand how your own time is for you too.

To do your daily practice.
To do it for you too.

To understand how you are worthy and deserving to receive.
You are worthy and deserving to receive your own time too.

It takes Time.
It takes your own time too.

Because it has been a long time you have held onto these thoughts about you.
It has been a long time you have thought these thoughts too.

Including the Thought that makes you think you don't have enough Time.
Including the Thought that makes you think there is never enough time to do what you want to do too.

But every time you receive the Understanding, you understand what your mind can also do.
So the next time your mind gets stuck in a loop, you understand how to break the cycle of thoughts too.

Because every time you receive your own understanding, you are mastering your own mind.

By choosing to shift your mind from the Thinking to the Understanding.
By choosing to expand your mind to include the Understanding too.

To focus on how it simply is.
To focus on how it simply is for you too.

Because you understand what your mind is doing when it gets stuck in a thought.
You understand what your mind is doing when it gets stuck in your own thought about you.

And every time you do, you are growing.

You are growing out of your own head.
Because you are outgrowing your own thoughts about you.

And growing deeper in your own understanding.
To grow rooted in the Understanding of how it has nothing to
do with you.

Because We Are All Still Learning.
They are still learning too.

Learning how to receive the Understanding of how We Are All
Still Learning.
To receive your own understanding of how you are still
learning too.

So there can be no blame.
Not even of you.

There can be no shame.
No shame of anything you are too.

Because we all make mistakes.
You make mistakes too.

Because we are all experiencing who we are for the first time.
And so are you.

Which is why mistakes are shared experiences.
When you own up to what you do.

To receive the Understanding of another.
Because they understand too.

Because they have made mistakes.
Because they are still learning too.

Which is why there is nothing to be forgiven.
And nothing to redo.

Because the only way you would have arrived here is from every experience.
Every experience in the Experience of You.

So you can see it too.
See how there is nothing to be forgiven.

Because We Are All Still Learning.
You are still learning too.

Learning how to receive this Understanding.
Receive this Understanding for you too.

To see how no one ever meant to hurt you.
They were simply hurting too.

Because they didn't know what else to do.
Other than keep hurting them with their own thoughts too.

Which is why you kept hurting.
Because you didn't know what else you could do too.

And now you do.

Because you understand everything you own mind can also do.
You understand everything your own mind can do for you too.

Because you understand how to release the Thought.
To release who you are too.

Because you are not a thought.
You simply are.

And you are here.
Right here.

Exactly where you need to be.
Exactly where you want to be too.

Because you are experiencing it.
You are experiencing it right now too.

How the Mind receives.
How your mind receives too.

So you can simply be.

Be here too.

To return to the Balance.
To see the Wholeness too.

See everything it is.
See how everything has been for you too.

Every experience.
Every experience in the Experience of You.

To arrive at the Understanding.
To return to the Understanding of You.

The natural cycle of Arriving and Returning.
The natural cycle of who you are too.

It was simply a habit your mind got conditioned to do.
Think.
Rather than simply be.

Which is how your mind learned to think about you.
Rather than simply allow you to be who you are too.

Because this is simply how it is.
This is simply how it is for you too.

The Experience of Who You Are.
The Experience of You.

A natural unfolding.
A gradual revealing.
A constant returning.

The natural unfolding of all the layers of thoughts that kept
you hidden.
The natural unfolding of all the layers of thoughts that kept
you blocked.
Even from you.

To gradually reveal everything you are.
Everything you already are.
Everything you have always been too.

From the constant returning.
The constant returning here.
To the Understanding.

The Understanding of how your mind can do this for you too.
To understand how it was never about you.
It was always for you too.

For you to learn how to receive.
Receive the Understanding.
Receive your own understanding too.

And it simply arrives.
When you simply allow the Thought to arrive too.

Because you are no longer afraid of the Thought.
Because you see the gift your own thoughts are giving you.

To master your own mind.
To see your mind as your best friend too.

And it takes Time.
It takes your own time too.

And Time can be used to heal your own thoughts.
Your time can be used to heal your own thoughts too.

So as you continue to experience who you are for the first time, you are grounded.
Rooted.
Confident.
Secure.

Confident and secure in who you are too.

So the next time your thoughts make you feel insecure, you understand why it is happening.

The next time your own thoughts make you feel insecure about you, you understand it is also happening for you too.

For you to learn how to receive the Understanding.
Rather than get stuck in the loop that makes you think something is wrong with you.

To understand how your feelings are natural.
How your feelings are true.

Because your feelings reflect the Truth.
The Truth of You.

And how you are feeling right now.
How you are feeling right now about you.

So rather than be afraid to feel what you do, sit in the Feeling.

So your mind can detach the Thought you learned to attach to the feeling.
So you can simply feel the way you do.

To understand how there is nothing wrong with feeling.
Because your feelings guide you to the thoughts that keep making you feel the way you do.

It is the Thought that makes you feel lonely.
Your own thought about you.
That makes you think you are all alone.

And now you understand how to receive the Understanding too.

To understand how you are never alone in this thought.
Because we all learn to think this thought about who we are too.

It is the Thought that makes you feel guilty.
Your own thought about you.
That makes you think you did something wrong.

And now you understand how to receive the Understanding too.

To understand how We Are All Still Learning.
They are still learning.
And you are still learning too.

It is the Thought that makes you feel angry.
Your own thought about you.
That makes you think someone wronged you.

And now you understand how to receive the Understanding
too.

To understand how easy it is to misunderstand.
When you are stuck in a thought.
When they are stuck in a thought too.

It is the Thought that makes you feel ashamed.
Your own thought about you.
That makes you think you need to be ashamed about any part
of you.

And now you understand how to receive the Understanding
too.

To understand how to see the Wholeness.
The Wholeness of everything that makes you *you*.

And why there is no comparison.
Because only you can be you.

So you are no longer afraid to feel.
Because you understand how the Feeling will pass too.

Which is why every storm passes.
Why your feelings pass too.

Simply how the Experience is.
Simply how the Experience of You is too.

So you can feel again.

Feel alive.
Feel free.
Feel who you are too.

So you can enjoy the experience.
So you can enjoy the Experience of You too.

Because you understand.
You understand how it is for you too.

The Sadness isn't here to hurt you.
The Sadness arrives so the Joy can arrive too.

The Sadness isn't here to break you.
The Sadness returns so the Joy can return too.

Because the Joy is part of the Experience of You.
To return you to the Balance.
To feel whole and complete with who you are too.

Which is why you have Tears of Sadness.
And Tears of Joy too.

For you to learn how to release.
Release who you are too.

Because you are not a thought.

You are the master of your own mind.
Which is why the Mind can learn how to do this.
Why your own mind can learn how to do this too.

Simply how it is.
Simply how it is for you too.

A natural cycle of Arriving and Returning.
A natural cycle of returning to your own understanding too.

So you can be at peace.

At peace in your own mind.
At peace in your own heart.

At peace with how it is.
At peace with who you are too.

So you can end the Struggle.
You can stop the Fight.

And live in the Understanding.
Live in your own light.

So every day gets lighter.
Because your mind is getting lighter too.

Because you keep releasing the weight of your own thoughts.
The darkness of your own thoughts too.

Because you understand.

You understand how your mind has never been against you.
Your mind isn't here to fight you too.

Your mind is simply here.
Waiting to learn what you want it to do for you too.

Because We Are All Still Learning.
Your mind is still learning too.

To understand how to begin from the Understanding.
Rather than from the Thought.

To keep returning to who you are.
Who you already are.
Who you have always been too.

Because you understand.
Because your mind understands too.

Which is why it always begins from the Understanding.

Because one Moment of Understanding returns you to the Understanding of everything your mind can also do.

One moment of your own understanding returns you to the Understanding of everything your mind has been waiting to do for you too.

5. The Who

You are here.
You have always been here.
Waiting patiently for you to return here too.

Because when you are here, *you* are here.
Present.
In the Presence of You.

So you are filled.
Filled with the Understanding too.

The Understanding of Who You Are.
The Understanding of You.

The Void was never real.
The Void was simply the Absence of You.

A thought you learned to think about you.
That made you think something was missing.

You were simply missing you.

Who you are.
Who you already are too.

The Void was simply a thought that made you think you were incomplete.

It is the Thought that was incomplete.
And now you understand how to complete the Thought for you too.

Because only you can complete you.

Which is why no amount of food, exercise, work, distractions could fill the Void.
Because the Void was simply the Absence of You.

And there can be no Absence in the Presence.
There can be no Absence in the Presence of You.

Which is why you are never alone when you are here.
You are never alone when you are with you.

Because you are someone too.

And you see it.
You see it now too.

Because you see you in a new light.
Because you see the Light too.

The Darkness wasn't meant to hurt you.
The Darkness was to help you see.

See how the Darkness is simply the Absence of Light.

And now you understand how your mind can shine a light on the Darkness too.

Because you understand how the Darkness was simply created by you.
And your own thoughts.

The thoughts you learned to think about you.
The thoughts someone else made you learn to think too.

Which is why your mind can also receive.
Receive this Understanding too.

To see the Light.
To return to the Lightness too.

The Lightness of Being.
Being here.
With who you are too.

In your presence.
The Presence of You.

So you are no longer thinking.
You are no longer thinking about you.

You are no longer thinking about your self.
Your image.
Your story.

You are simply here.
Simply being.

Being who you are.
Who you have always been too.

No thought required.

How you are is not the same as who you are.
How you are is based on all the experiences you have had so
far in the Experience of You.
And how you learned to think about them.

Which is how your mind learned to think about you.
And how you are right now too.

Who you are is your presence.
Which is why you have always been here.
Waiting patiently for you to return here too.

To experience what it means.
To experience it for you too.

What it means to simply be here.
What it means to simply be too.

So you can feel the release.
Your mind releasing you.

From all the thoughts that kept you hidden.
From all the thoughts that kept you imprisoned too.

So you can be freed.
Free to simply be.

Simply be here.
Receiving the Understanding too.

Because you understand how it simply is.
How it simply is for you too.

How your mind will wander.
How your mind will drift.
How your mind will be filled with thoughts too.

And now you understand how your mind can focus.
How your mind can shift.
How your mind can empty from the Understanding too.

Because you hear it.

You hear the Understanding arriving.
You hear the Understanding returning too.

Because this is what your mind is doing every time a thought arrives.
This is what your mind is doing now for you too.

Because you feel it.

You feel the shift.
When your mind shifts from the Thinking to the Understanding.

Because you feel it for you too.

The Peace.
The Calm.
The Comfort.
The Lightness and Joy too.

When your mind shifts from your own thoughts to your own understanding of you.

Because you understand.
You understand everything your mind can also do.

To understand how you can be proud of who you are.
And love who you are too.

So every day, this is what you carry with you too.

Your own understanding.
The Understanding of You.

So you are filled.
And your days are fulfilled too.

Because you understand how your mind can also receive.
Receive this Understanding too.

So the only thing you can do is live in the Thank You.

Because you understand the gift your thoughts are giving you too.

To return you here.
To this moment.
So you can be in this moment with who you are too.

Which is why Life unfolds Moment to Moment.
Why your life unfolds moment to moment too.

Because within each moment is the gift.
For you to receive too.

No matter what you think you have done.
No matter what you think about you.

Within each moment is the gift.
The Gift of the Understanding.
Your own understanding too.

To understand why.
Why you are too.

Why you are worthy and deserving to receive.
Worthy and deserving to be here too.

To see how it was never a matter of becoming.
It is a matter of returning.

Returning here.
To this moment.
To receive the Understanding that has always been available
for you too.

So no matter what happens, you understand why it is
happening too.
To learn how to receive.
Receive the Understanding for you too.

You didn't do anything wrong.
Your mind simply got conditioned to think this way about
you.

You aren't to blame.
Your mind simply didn't understand yet how to receive the
Understanding of how We Are All Still Learning.
How you are still learning too.

Learning how to own up to your own thoughts.
And be responsible for what you are doing too.

Learning how your own mind can do this.
Within each moment of the Experience of You.

This is the Balance.
This is the Wholeness.
This is the Wholeness of everything your own mind can also
do.

To understand how to return.
How to keep returning too.

The natural cycle of Arriving and Returning.
The natural cycle of returning to this moment too.

So you can live Moment to Moment.
And enjoy the experience too.

The Experience of Who You Are.
The Experience of You.

Because you understand what you are doing.
And what you can do for you too.

So you are no longer afraid of what you don't know.
Because you understand how the next moment is unknown.
Even for you.

So you are no longer afraid of the Unknown.
Because you know what your mind can also do.

Because you understand you are still learning.
You understand this for you too.

So you can keep letting go of how you think it should be.
To enjoy the experience of how it simply is too.

You can keep letting go of how you think you should be.
To enjoy the experience of who you simply are too.

Because this moment is all you need.
All you need to return here too.

And it simply arrives.
When you simply allow it to arrive too.

So allow the Thought to arrive.
So the Understanding can arrive too.

Simply allow the Thought to return.
To return to the Understanding too.

The Understanding of Who You Are.
The Understanding of You.

To understand how you are enough.
Just the way you are too.

Which is why Life only made one of you.

You can keep denying this Truth with your own thoughts.
You can keep deluding you and deceiving you too.

But this is simply the Truth.
The Truth of Who You Are too.

Because no matter what you say, no matter what you do,
no matter what you think, it holds true.

Because only you can do what only you can do.
Be you.

The only you there is.
The only you there will ever be.

You are allowed to live in this Understanding too.
So you can feel again.
Feel who you are too.

Your breath.
Your presence.
Why people love you.

Who you are.
Who you already are.
Who you have always been too.

Because you are allowed to live in the Understanding.
Your own understanding too.

Which is why your mind can also receive.
So you can receive everything Life has to offer.

Everything your life has to offer you.
Everything your life has to offer others too.

To do your part.
To make your contribution too.

Because when you are present, you are participating.

You are participating in Life.
You are participating in your own life too.

Because you are sharing your presence.

Sharing your presence with the world.
Sharing it with you too.

Because your participation is required.
Because you are included too.

Which is why you are here.
Why your mind can return you here too.

So you can feel it.
How it makes you feel too.

When you live in the Understanding.
When someone understands you too.

To see how you didn't do anything wrong.
You are still learning too.

Learning how to receive your own understanding.
To understand how you are worthy and deserving too.

To be proud of who you are.
Confident and secure in who you are too.

To love you for you.
As you already are too.

Which is why it always begins from the Understanding.

Because one Moment of Understanding is enough for your mind to return here too.

One moment of your own understanding is enough for your mind to return you to you.

This is the Purejoojoo Guide to the Understanding.
The Understanding of everything the Mind can do.
Everything your own mind can do for you too.

Because you are the master of your own mind.
Your thoughts don't master you.

Thank you for being who you are too.

6. The Journal Pages

Every morning, read the Understanding in your mind.

So your mind learns how to receive.
Receive the Understanding of everything your mind can do.
Everything your mind can do for you too.

Then receive Three Full Cycles of Breath.

So you can feel it.
How it feels to be complete.
Completed by you.
Being completely here.
Being completely present.
In the Presence of Who You Are.
Who you already are too.

Every afternoon, at 3:00 p.m., you will simply listen and receive.

Sign up at www.purejoojoo.com to receive the Three Minute Purejoojoo Guided Breathing Experience.
To experience what it means to empty your mind.
To experience how your mind can simply be empty too.
To relax into your being.
Being here.
Being you.

Every evening, write out the Understanding.

So you can see it.
So your mind can see it too.
See how the Understanding makes sense.
How it makes sense for you too.

Then read the Understanding out loud.

With your own voice.
So your mind can hear it.
So you can hear it too.

Then receive Three Full Cycles of Breath.

So you can feel it.
Your breath.
Your presence.
You.

We Are All Still Learning. I am still learning too. Learning how to receive. Receive my own understanding of how I am worthy and deserving to receive too. As I am. As I already am too. Thank you. Thank you. Thank you.

We Are All Still Learning. I am still learning too. Learning how to receive the Understanding of how there can be no blame. There can be no shame. When we are all still learning. They are still learning. And I am too. Thank you. Thank you. Thank you.

We Are All Still Learning. I am still learning too. Learning how to receive. Receive my own understanding of how I am worthy and deserving to receive Love too. Including my own love. Because Love is meant for me too. Thank you. Thank you. Thank you.

We Are All Still Learning. I am still learning too. Learning how to stop comparing. Because I am enough. I have always been enough. Because there is such thing as Enough. Which is why only I can do what only I can do. Be who I am. Who I already am too. Thank you. Thank you. Thank you.

We Are All Still Learning. I am still learning too. Learning how to receive. Receive my own understanding too. The Understanding that I am never alone when I am here. Because I am someone too. Thank you. Thank you. Thank you.

We Are All Still Learning. I am still learning too. Learning how to receive. Receive my own understanding too. The Understanding of how I matter. How I am included. How I belong here too. Which is why I am here. Why I am already here. Right here. Exactly where I need to be. Exactly where I want to be too. Thank you. Thank you. Thank you.

We Are All Still Learning. I am still learning too. Learning how to receive. Receive my own understanding too. The Understanding of how I am allowed to receive everything Life has to offer. Because I am worthy and deserving to receive too. Thank you. Thank you. Thank you.

We Are All Still Learning. I am still learning too. Learning how to receive. Receive my own understanding too. To let go of the thoughts that make me feel the way I do. And let in all the Love that has always been here for me too. Thank you. Thank you. Thank you.

We Are All Still Learning. I am still learning too. Learning how to receive. Receive my own understanding too. To stop comparing who I am. Because there can be no comparison when it comes to who I am. Because I am the only one who can be who I am. And I am proud to be who I am too. Thank you. Thank you. Thank you.

We Are All Still Learning. I am still learning too. Learning how to receive. Receive my own understanding too. Because my mind can also do this. Do this for me too. Because I am the master of my own mind. My mind is my best friend too. Thank you. Thank you. Thank you.

We Are All Still Learning. I am still learning too. Learning how to stop fighting. Fighting against who I am. Who I already am too. And I am not my thoughts. I simply am. And I am allowed to receive this Understanding for me too. Thank you. Thank you. Thank you.

We Are All Still Learning. I am still learning too. Learning how to receive. Receive my own understanding of how I am worthy and deserving to receive too. As I am. As I already am too. Thank you. Thank you. Thank you.

We Are All Still Learning. I am still learning too. Learning how to receive the Understanding of how there can be no blame. There can be no shame. When we are all still learning. They are still learning. And I am too. Thank you. Thank you. Thank you.

We Are All Still Learning. I am still learning too. Learning how to receive. Receive my own understanding of how I am worthy and deserving to receive Love too. Including my own love. Because Love is meant for me too. Thank you. Thank you. Thank you.

We Are All Still Learning. I am still learning too. Learning how to stop comparing. Because I am enough. I have always been enough. Because there is such thing as Enough. Which is why only I can do what only I can do. Be who I am. Who I already am too. Thank you. Thank you. Thank you.

We Are All Still Learning. I am still learning too. Learning how to receive. Receive my own understanding too. The Understanding that I am never alone when I am here. Because I am someone too. Thank you. Thank you. Thank you.

We Are All Still Learning. I am still learning too. Learning how to receive. Receive my own understanding too. The Understanding of how I matter. How I am included. How I belong here too. Which is why I am here. Why I am already here. Right here. Exactly where I need to be. Exactly where I want to be too. Thank you. Thank you. Thank you.

We Are All Still Learning. I am still learning too. Learning how to receive. Receive my own understanding too. The Understanding of how I am allowed to receive everything Life has to offer. Because I am worthy and deserving to receive too. Thank you. Thank you. Thank you.

We Are All Still Learning. I am still learning too. Learning how to receive. Receive my own understanding too. To let go of the thoughts that make me feel the way I do. And let in all the Love that has always been here for me too. Thank you. Thank you. Thank you.

We Are All Still Learning. I am still learning too. Learning how to receive. Receive my own understanding too. To stop comparing who I am. Because there can be no comparison when it comes to who I am. Because I am the only one who can be who I am. And I am proud to be who I am too. Thank you. Thank you. Thank you.

We Are All Still Learning. I am still learning too. Learning how to receive. Receive my own understanding too. Because my mind can also do this. Do this for me too. Because I am the master of my own mind. My mind is my best friend too. Thank you. Thank you. Thank you.

We Are All Still Learning. I am still learning too. Learning how to stop fighting. Fighting against who I am. Who I already am too. And I am not my thoughts. I simply am. And I am allowed to receive this Understanding for me too. Thank you. Thank you. Thank you.

We Are All Still Learning. I am still learning too. Learning how to receive. Receive my own understanding of how I am worthy and deserving to receive too. As I am. As I already am too. Thank you. Thank you. Thank you.

We Are All Still Learning. I am still learning too. Learning how to receive the Understanding of how there can be no blame. There can be no shame. When we are all still learning. They are still learning. And I am too. Thank you. Thank you. Thank you.

We Are All Still Learning. I am still learning too. Learning how to receive. Receive my own understanding of how I am worthy and deserving to receive Love too. Including my own love. Because Love is meant for me too. Thank you. Thank you. Thank you.

We Are All Still Learning. I am still learning too. Learning how to stop comparing. Because I am enough. I have always been enough. Because there is such thing as Enough. Which is why only I can do what only I can do. Be who I am. Who I already am too. Thank you. Thank you. Thank you.

We Are All Still Learning. I am still learning too. Learning how to receive. Receive my own understanding too. The Understanding that I am never alone when I am here. Because I am someone too. Thank you. Thank you. Thank you.

We Are All Still Learning. I am still learning too. Learning how to receive. Receive my own understanding too. The Understanding of how I matter. How I am included. How I belong here too. Which is why I am here. Why I am already here. Right here. Exactly where I need to be. Exactly where I want to be too. Thank you. Thank you. Thank you.

We Are All Still Learning. I am still learning too. Learning how to receive. Receive my own understanding too. The Understanding of how I am allowed to receive everything Life has to offer. Because I am worthy and deserving to receive too. Thank you. Thank you. Thank you.

We Are All Still Learning. I am still learning too. Learning how to receive. Receive my own understanding too. To let go of the thoughts that make me feel the way I do. And let in all the Love that has always been here for me too. Thank you. Thank you. Thank you.

We Are All Still Learning. I am still learning too. Learning how to receive. Receive my own understanding too. To stop comparing who I am. Because there can be no comparison when it comes to who I am. Because I am the only one who can be who I am. And I am proud to be who I am too. Thank you. Thank you. Thank you.

We Are All Still Learning. I am still learning too. Learning how to receive. Receive my own understanding too. Because my mind can also do this. Do this for me too. Because I am the master of my own mind. My mind is my best friend too. Thank you. Thank you. Thank you.

We Are All Still Learning. I am still learning too. Learning how to stop fighting. Fighting against who I am. Who I already am too. And I am not my thoughts. I simply am. And I am allowed to receive this Understanding for me too. Thank you. Thank you. Thank you.

7. The Blank Pages

These pages are empty.
For you to experience the Emptiness too.

So you can simply be.
So your mind can be empty too.

Take a moment to sit in the Emptiness of the blank pages.
So your mind can expand to include the Understanding too.

The Understanding of how everything is possible when the Mind is empty.
Everything is possible for you when your own mind is empty too.

And when you are ready, start to release.
Release how you feel.

By writing it all down.
Writing it all out.
So you can let it all out too.

And once you are done, complete the Release from the Understanding.

By writing out an Understanding.
From one of the Journal Pages.
Which are all for you too.

For your mind to understand how to release the Thought.
So you can feel the Release too.

Don't be afraid to experience everything you feel.
Because you can always return.

Return here.
To the Understanding.

Which is always here.

Just return to the start of the book.
To return to the Understanding.

Until you can release the book too.

Because the Mind will simply understand.
Your mind will simply understand too.

How to empty.
Empty to receive.

Receive everything that has always been here.
Waiting for you to learn how to receive it too.

From the Understanding.
From your own understanding of who you are too.

Because you are the master of your own mind.
Your mind can do this for you too.

.

8. Daily Purejoojoo Reminders

The next few pages are daily reminders for you too.

To remember everything you are.

Everything you already are too.

Put one on your bathroom mirror.

So every morning, you can see it for you too.

Who you are.

And why you are already enough as you are too.

And then you decide where you want to put the other reminders.

Because you always get to decide for you too.

How you want to experience you.

How you want to experience your own mind too.

I am enough.
Just the way I am too.
I have always been enough.
As I already am too.

.

I love who I am.
I am proud of who I am.
Because I am allowed
to be proud of who I am too.

There is no comparision
When it comes to who I am.
Because I am *who I am.*
And I am allowed
to be who I am too.

I am exactly where I need to be.
Everything is happening
as it should.
Everything.

This feeling will pass.
I am simply
breaking out of the thought.
I am breaking me out of
this pattern of thought too.

I am worthy and deserving
to receive
the Understanding too.

We Are All Still Learning.
I am still learning too.

I am loved.
I have always been loved.
Because
my love is meant for me too.

I am never alone
when I am here.
Because I am someone too.

I matter.
I belong.
Because I am included too.
Which is why I am here.
Because I was given life too.

I am allowed
to be seen and heard as me.
Who I am.
Who I already am too.

I am
the master of my own mind.
My thoughts
don't master me.

9. Acknowledgements

I am who I am because of you.

And every person I have met so far in the Experience of Who I Am too.

Beginning with my parents.

My beautiful mother who continues to teach me every day what it means to love.

And be loved too.

My sweet gentle father whose presence is always with me.

Guiding me to the Understanding that he will always be here with me too.

My incredible sister.

Who showed me what it means to live your own life.

And what it means to decide for me too.

My sweet nephew.

Who makes my heart explode with such Joy.

And reminds me to keep returning to the Innocence and Wonder too.

My amazing friends.

Who understand how I am.

And who I am too.

My lovely.

The man I met up in the air.

In a plane above the clouds.

Who allowed me to receive.

And express it out loud too.

And every other person I have met so far.

And yet to meet too.

For teaching me how We Are All Still Learning.

For helping me see how I am still learning too.

And to you.

For simply listening and receiving.

Receiving what I have to say.

And who I am too.

Thank you for being here.

Thank you. Thank you. Thank you.

ADDITIONAL RESOURCES

Available at www.purejoojoo.com

Including the audio version of the book.

Made in the USA
Middletown, DE
24 September 2019